YOUTH BIBLE STUDY GUIDE

Father God

His Love, Power, Grace and Will

Youth Bible Study Guides

Sexuality

Following God

Image and Self-Esteem

Peer Pressure

Father God

Jesus Christ and the Holy Spirit

Sin, Forgiveness and Eternal Life

Church, Prayer and Worship

Sharing Your Faith

Tough Times

Money and Giving

Hunger, Poverty and Justice

YOUTH BIBLE STUDY GUIDE

Father God

His Love, Power, Grace and Will

COMPILED AND WRITTEN BY
CHIP AND HELEN KENDALL

Authentic

Copyright © 2014 Chip and Helen Kendall

20 19 18 17 16 15 14   7 6 5 4 3 2 1

First published 2014 by Authentic Media Ltd
Presley Way, Crownhill, Milton Keynes, MK8 0ES.
www.authenticmedia.co.uk

The right of Chip and Helen Kendall to be identified as the Authors of this Work
has been asserted by them in accordance with the
Copyright, Designs and Patents Act 1988.

British Library Cataloguing in Publication Data
A catalogue record for this book is available from the British Library

ISBN-13: 978-1-86024-632-6

Scripture quotations are taken from the Holy Bible: Easy-to-Read Version™, Anglicized.
Copyright © 2013 World Bible Translation Center,
a subsidiary of Bible League International.

Extracts taken from:
Steve Adams, *The Word Through Sound*, Authentic 2004
Andy Frost and Jo Wells, *Freestyle*, Authentic, 2005
Chip Kendall, *The Mind of chipK: Enter at Your Own Risk*, Authentic, 2005
Vince Woltjer and Tim Vandenberg, *To Be Honest With You*, Authentic, 2005
Amanda Lord and Simon Lord, *Search for a Father*, Authentic, 2006
Shell Perris, *Something to Shout About*, Authentic, 2006

Cover and page design by Temple Design
Cover based on a design by Beth Ellis
Printed in Great Britain by Bell and Bain, Glasgow

Since you are now God's children,
he has sent the Spirit of his Son into your hearts.
The Spirit cries out, '*Abba*, Father'.
(Galatians 4:6)

Chip and Helen Kendall are Creative Arts Pastors at Audacious Church, Manchester, and also love spending as much time as possible with their kids, Cole, Eden and Elliot. They currently reside in Stockport, England and they still have trouble understanding each other's accents.

Chip tours the world, fronting the Chip Kendall band. His album *Holy Freaks* and first book, *The Mind of chipK: Enter at Your Own Risk* has helped loads of young people grow in their faith. He's also the driving force behind a new youth media movement called MYvoice with Cross Rhythms, as well as being a regular presenter on GodTV. All of these jobs continue to pave the way for him to speak at events everywhere. www.chipkendall.com

After working for ten years as a dancer and tour/bookings manager, Helen now juggles looking after the kids with her work at Audacious Church helping to develop dance and all things creative. She also enjoys doing some writing and project management. Helen loves the variety in her life, and no two days are ever the same.

Guest writer, Ben Jack
Through his role as director of the resourcing organization Generation Now, and as a speaker and author, Ben is committed to helping youth and young adults question, evaluate, understand and live for a faith in Jesus. Ben is passionate about exploring narrative – particularly through film – and the role of story in our faith and lives, as well as culture, philosophy and theology. Ben is also known as award-winning DJ & producer Galactus Jack. www.ben-jack.com / www.generation-now.co.uk

Thank Yous

Massive thanks to Malcolm Down, Liz Williams and the rest of the gang at Authentic Media for giving us the opportunity to work on these study guides . . . it's been a blast. To everyone at SFC who read the books and gave us your thoughts, we appreciate the feedback. Thanks to everyone at Audacious Church for being an amazing church family. Thanks to lovely Lucy West for the fantastic photos and Lucy Wells for the typing. To everyone who talked to Chip for the 'people clips', thanks for your honesty and willingness to put up with the quirky questions. A really huge thank you to our dads for their 'father knows best' wisdom. We loved your perspective on things. Finally, big thanks to all the authors whose work we have used in this book. You are an inspiration.

CONTENTS

INSTRUCTIONS

The book you're holding in your hands is a study guide. It's a compilation of extracts from lots of other books written about this subject. It might not make you the world's expert on the subject, but it should give you lots of useful information and, even better, it should give you some idea of what the Bible has to say about . . .
FATHER GOD: HIS LOVE, POWER, GRACE AND WILL.

What is a 'reaction box'?

Throughout the book, you'll find these helpful little reaction boxes. We've added them so that you can decide for yourself what you think about what you've just read. Here's what one should look like once you've filled it in:

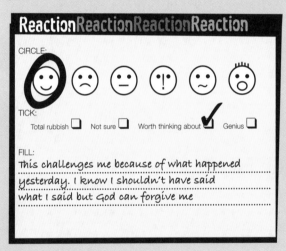

Pretty simple really . . .

Circle the face that reflects how you feel about it.

Tick the box that shows what you think about it.

Fill in any thoughts you have about what you've learned on the lines provided.

What are 'people clips'?

Just so you don't get too bored, we've added a bunch of 'people clips' to each study guide. These are people just like you, who were happy for us to pick their brains about various related topics. Who knows? Maybe you'll find someone you recognize.

What is 'father knows best'?

In a book about the father-heart of God, we couldn't resist including some great tips from the legends that are . . . our fathers. Roy (Chip's dad) and Adrian (Helen's dad) were kind enough to contribute some fantastic advice, so read it with great care. Oh, and ignore the stories about bath time.

What is a 'reality check'?

Finally, throughout the book you will come across sections called 'Reality check'. These should provide a chance for you to apply what you've been learning to your own life experiences.

Other than that, the only rule that applies when reading this book is that you HAVE FUN! So start reading.

Chip & Helen

Introduction
Who's the DADDY?

Rob had no memory of his real father. He'd died of cancer shortly after Rob was born, and now he was with the angels in heaven. But this never really bothered Rob because his mum had re-married less than four years after the tragedy, and Rob's step-dad was the only dad he'd ever known.

O n his thirteenth birthday, after all the presents had been opened and all the cake had been eaten, Rob's mother handed him something that he would come to cherish as one of the greatest gifts he'd ever been given. **IT WAS A LARGE ENVELOPE, STUFFED WITH LETTERS WRITTEN TO HIM BY HIS REAL DAD** during the months before his death. It was his dad's way of leaving something behind so that Rob could get to know him, since he knew he didn't have much time left.

Rob didn't read all the letters at once. After all, to begin with it was no different to reading something given to him by a complete stranger. As far as Rob was concerned, he had a good dad already – his step-dad. Even though his mum had told him stories about his real father, Rob never thought about him all that much. But over the course of time, sometimes through blurry tears and sometimes through fits of laughter, he came to know and love this 'invisible father' who'd poured so much of himself into these simple letters.

Rob learned that his real dad was very similar to his step-dad in a lot of ways, yet completely opposite in others. Each letter brought him a new and different understanding of who his real father was. His stories and advice, his hopes and fears, and the plans and dreams he had for his newborn son. Best of all, every single one of them finished with the words, 'I love you forever.' These particular words, written in his father's own handwriting, seemed to jump off of the page and straight into his heart. It made him want to be a better person somehow . . .

Are you hooked on this story yet? We hope you are. Throughout this book you'll find excerpts from some of the letters Rob's dad wrote to him. These excerpts are called 'Dear Rob . . .' and we hope you really find them helpful.

In some ways, these letters that Rob's dad wrote to him are a bit like the Bible is to us. The Bible might not read like a letter or a story all the time but, nevertheless, throughout history God has inspired some very good writers to put ink to paper so that we can get to know him a little bit better. And even though God is 'invisible', his characteristics can be seen all around us in his creation. The wind, the sun, the oceans – even electricity. Plus, the Bible clearly shows us that God is eternal. Rob's dad may have died of cancer, but our heavenly Dad is just as alive now as ever!

When it comes to thinking about God as our heavenly Father, a really good place to start is with our earthly dads. If you were to be specific, **HOW WOULD YOU DESCRIBE THE ROLE YOUR OWN FATHER HAS IN YOUR LIFE?** Provider? Authority figure? Loving? Protective? Over-protective? Royal pain in the butt?

Maybe, like Rob, you've never even met your dad. Or your parents are divorced, so you don't get to see him very often. Maybe you've had an abusive dad, in which case you struggle to even think of anything remotely good when it comes to the topic of fatherhood. Whatever your story is, this book is written with the express purpose of helping you see the Father-heart of God – specifically his love, power, grace and will.

At times it might be helpful to think of the example your earthly father has given you, and at other times you'll just have to remember that no matter how hard your dad tries – he's not perfect. Not as perfect as God anyway. God is the perfect Dad. He is truly all-powerful and his love is unconditional.

So let's see what the Bible has to say about . . . *Father God: His Love, Power, Grace and Will.*

The Father's Love

The Father himself loves you because you have loved me.
And he loves you because you have believed
that I came from God.

(John 16:27)

1

First up

The Bible describes God as many things. Here are just a few of them: a king, a shepherd, a teacher, a farmer, a judge, a priest, a landlord – even a mother hen! But no list of God's biblical attributes (even a short one) would be complete without mentioning him as a loving Father.

The roles listed above are all good descriptions of someone who has a lot of authority and responsibility, and the things they're in charge of are all readily recognizable by anyone living in the 21st century. Sheep, students, seeds, convicts, chickens, etc. But when it comes to understanding God's desire to have a meaningful loving relationship with us . . . well, you just can't beat knowing him as Dad.

For a lot of people, the word 'dad' automatically conjures up images of the lovely, cosy, simple things that define any earthly dad and what he does (or doesn't do) for them. But if you think the love your natural dad has for you is something special, just wait until you get a revelation of your heavenly Dad's love. God's love is unconditional, relentless and 100% foolproof. He kisses us with each new sunrise. He sings his convicting words straight into our hearts. When our spirits are crushed, he resuscitates us with his life-giving breath. His loving hands literally transform our character to be more like his perfect Son. If Jesus is the King of kings and Lord of lords, then surely Father God is the Dad of dads.

This first Life Lesson zooms in on God's love for us. We think it'll make a great foundation for you to build upon as we move on to unpacking his power, his grace and his will. Remember that God doesn't change. He is love. It's his motivation for everything – especially when it comes to executing his power, grace and will. That's just as real and true now as it ever was in Bible times, and it will continue to ring true long after our time on this earth is finished. But don't just take our word for it. Read on and decide for yourself.

Live to Love

Ben talks

When I was 10 years old, I was told that I would need to start wearing glasses (by an optician, not just some random guy on the street!). At first it seemed a bit of a drag, having this strange metal frame on my face all the time. After a few weeks, though, I stopped noticing them. These days I don't really ever think about my glasses, they're just there, helping me to see clearly.

I recently broke my glasses by accident while I was out with some friends. I realized that without them I can't see very much, and so driving home was no longer an option! In that moment it became clear just how important my glasses are to my daily life.

Day by day we can fall into the trap of forgetting how essential God's love is to our lives. Breaking or losing my glasses is inconvenient, but living life to the full without recognizing and embracing God's amazing love is impossible!

Read 1 John 4:7–21. See also Deuteronomy 7:9, John 3:16–21, Galatians 2:20.

Reflect

- *What do the verses in 1 John 4 teach you about God's love and what our response to it should be?*

- *Do you see this kind of love demonstrated in the world around you? How could you change that by embracing God's love afresh each day?*

Respond

- *Think about how you can live fully in God's love this week, and then get practical in demonstrating that love to people around you.*

Remember

- *God's love is the key to living this life in all its fullness.*

ReactionReactionReactionReaction

CIRCLE:

TICK:

Total rubbish ☐   Not sure ☐   Worth thinking about ☑   Genius ☐

FILL:

It was good

Father knows best

When Helen was born I can remember being absolutely totally overwhelmed. It took me by surprise. There was a new person who was totally dependent and vulnerable, needing us to service it and completely needing our attention, love and care. I was totally besotted and in love with this new person, it was amazing.

Love Sick

Helen talks

Have you ever felt as if you had to be a certain way or do certain things in order to be loved? Do you feel that you have to do well at school, or look great, or be good at sports before you are accepted? Or have you ever wanted other people to do things or be a certain way before you would love them?

S ometimes we think, wrongly, that God's love for us comes with conditions. We can feel as if we have to be a perfect person in order for him to love us or accept us. It's really hard to believe that God loves us despite all our failings but it's TRUE!

The thing that has really helped me understand this is being a parent. Chip and I have three small, crazy little kids and I really do love them no matter what.

Once we were on a journey from South Africa to Manchester via Dubai (look at the map, that's a long flight!). Our little boy was about 6 months old and on the descent into Dubai (still another 8-hour flight to Manchester to go), while he was sitting on my knee, he filled his nappy to overflowing with the most enormous poo, which spilt onto my legs. How disgusting is that! Of course I had a change of clothes for *him*, but not for me. I don't know if you've ever looked for clothes in airports but it's mainly T-shirts and jumpers, not a lot of trousers on sale. So, needless to say, I smelt pretty bad on the flight back to Manchester.

Between them, my kids have been sick on me, kept me up all night, shouted, screamed, thrown the food I'd just made on the floor and all sorts of other things like that. But does that mean that I love them any less? Of course not! **MY LOVE ISN'T EARNED BY GOOD BEHAVIOUR**. They have it anyway. Obviously I'm pleased with them and proud of them when they do good things but it doesn't mean I don't love them if they mess up.

It's the same with God's love for us. I think if we could really get that to sink into our hearts and heads it would make a massive difference. You are loved, accepted, cherished and chosen by God. He is excited about you. Check out the verses below about how much God loves you:

This is how God showed his love to us: he sent his only Son into the world to give us life through him. True love is God's love for us, not our love for God. He sent his Son as the way to take away our sins. That is how much God loved us, dear friends! So we also must love each other.

(1 John 4:9–11)

But in all these troubles we have complete victory through God, who has shown his love for us. Yes, I am sure that nothing can separate us from God's love – not death or life, not angels or ruling spirits. I am sure that nothing now, nothing in the future, no powers, nothing above us or below us – nothing in the whole created world – will ever be able to separate us from the love God has shown us in Christ Jesus our Lord.

(Romans 8:37–39)

The LORD your God is with you. He is like a powerful soldier. He will save you. He will show how much he loves you and how happy he is with you. He will laugh and be happy about you.

(Zephaniah 3:17)

ReactionReactionReactionReaction

CIRCLE:

TICK:

Total rubbish ☐   Not sure ☐   Worth thinking about ☑   Genius ☐

FILL:

....

....

....

....

TOUGH LOVE

Chip talks

When a dad tells his teenage daughter she's not allowed to go out 'dressed like that', he's demonstrating tough love. She may hate him for a week, but he's got her entire future in mind.

When a coach demands a stricter regime from his star player than he does from the rest of his teammates, that's tough love. If that kid has what it takes, he'll be willing to make the sacrifice.

Tough love is selfless. It presumes the best. It seeks to develop character by prompting not just one good choice, but many great choices. It's in it for the long haul. It's not out to harm or humiliate, but it understands the phrase 'no pain, no gain'. It demonstrates true commitment. When the going gets tough, you'd better hope and pray that you're prepared for it, because somebody out there was willing to show you tough love.

Jesus also said in John 15:13, **'THE GREATEST LOVE PEOPLE CAN SHOW IS TO DIE FOR THEIR FRIENDS.'** This was clearly a reference to the way he was about to demonstrate his own love by dying on the cross, but I think it has another application as well. When we choose to put others and their needs first, ahead of ourselves or our own agendas, we're effectively dying to what we want so that what they want might spring to life. It's that same principle of sacrifice at work.

Take a few minutes to read Hebrews 12:5–11, then answer these questions:

- *Just like any good dad, what does God do to anyone he loves?*

- *If we accept our Heavenly Father's discipline, what does this passage promise that we will have?*

- *What are some ways that God has shown you tough love?*

- *Who are the people in your life that you can demonstrate tough, sacrificial love to today?*

CIRCLE:

TICK:

Total rubbish ☐   Not sure ☐   Worth thinking about ☑   Genius ☐

FILL:

....

....

Father knows best

Love has so many different aspects and every situation brings out a different one, whether it's through problems or good times, you discover a new aspect. I don't love my kids more when they are good than when they are bad. I just discover a father's unconditional love.

Name: **David Walters**

Age: **14**

Town: **Oxfordshire**

Current status: **Student**

Favourite subject in school:

P.E.

Have you ever spit-balled your teacher?

No.

What is the holiest thing you've ever done?

I don't think I've done anything holy, except go to church.

What do you think God is like?

Just some big guy in the sky. Don't really know.

How do you think you could find out?

By dying and going to heaven or having a vision.

What would you think of me, if I told you that God was your heavenly Father and he loves you very much?

I'd think you were telling the truth.

The Love of God

There is a lot of material to read here. If you are able, read the full account. If time is short read the abbreviated account:

Full account: Matthew 26:47 – 27:66

Abbreviated account: Matthew 27:32–61

Think about these questions:

- **If you were Jesus' mother, Mary, or one of the disciples watching Jesus die, would it seem like a demonstration of God's love?**

- **There's a song that says: 'My life had its beginning at your cross'. Do you think anyone watching Jesus' crucifixion saw it as a new start for them?**

- **What does this say about how we see things and how God sees things?**

YOUR VIEW?

There are two ways of looking at Jesus' death: as a believer or as a doubter. **Look at Matthew 26:14–16 and Matthew 26:28.** Judas was a doubter. He didn't see the bigger plan in it all. Jesus, however, knew there was a bigger purpose, which could only be fulfilled through his suffering. He believed.

The death of Jesus wasn't a random series of gruesome events. It was part of God's plan to bring us close to him – even though it was costly for him. This sort of love is called 'sacrificial love'.

SACRIFICIAL LOVE

Think about a time when you've been willing to accept a cost in order to show love to someone. Maybe you stayed up late one night looking after a sick family member, or spent time helping a friend with homework when you had other (more exciting) things planned. Why did you do it? What were you saying about the person through your actions?

Now think of a time when someone showed sacrificial love to you. How did it make you feel? What were they saying about you through their actions?

Now think about the death of Jesus. Jesus experienced fear, betrayal and anxiety:

- **Jesus was scared and didn't want to go through it (Matthew 26:39).**
- **Jesus' friends didn't do a good job in supporting him (Matthew 26:40–41).**
- **Jesus was betrayed at his weakest moment by a disciple (Matthew 26:47).**

However, something drove him on. What was it? Take a moment to think about this – in the face of fear and betrayal why didn't Jesus quit?

The answer is because of his love for you. Real love is always sacrificial love.

Think about yourself for a moment. Which description best fits you?

A **I find it easier to receive love than to give it.**

B **I find it easier to show love to others than to receive it.**

IF YOU ANSWERED A, READ THE FOLLOWING:

Jesus set his followers an example when he died. He showed a pattern for how Christians should love – sacrificially. And he showed that although loving other people is sometimes costly, God blesses us when we do it, and by doing it we prove our love is real.

Read Matthew 26:27–28.

Think about Jesus' example of what it means to love others sacrificially.

IF YOU ANSWERED B, READ THE FOLLOWING:

Jesus' death contains a strong message about how deeply he loves you.

Read Matthew 26:27–28.

Jesus gave the cup to everyone, symbolizing that they all needed to receive the sacrifice he was going to make in order to be forgiven and find true life.

Spend some time thinking: you need to receive Christ's love and sacrifice. Open your life to God. Talk to him about his love for you and ask him to help you receive it.

Steve Adams, *The Word Through Sound*, Authentic Media, 2004

ReactionReactionReactionReaction

CIRCLE:

TICK:

Total rubbish ☐   Not sure ☐   Worth thinking about ☐   Genius ☑

FILL:

....

....

....

....

Dear Rob,

I'll never forget being dumped for the very first time. I knew from the start that it couldn't last long, but that didn't stop me feeling like my whole world had been shattered.

I was fourteen. Her name was Emily and she was a year older than me. We'd actually only ever been on two official dates — once to the movies and once to a concert — but I thought about her constantly. I would do things for her that I never dreamed I'd ever do for anybody, like write poems and make her cards. Once I even bought a lotion that guaranteed to speed the growth of facial hair, all because I'd caught her staring at some model with stubble on his chin in a magazine!

Anyway, after school one day I went looking for Emily and found her behind the bus stop — kissing a guy from her class! I was absolutely gutted. Later that night, she rang me up and officially called it quits. At the time, I felt about as small as a flea. But as life goes on, you quickly learn that <u>many</u> things — not just girls — compete to win your heart and affections only to destroy them and leave you in pieces. All I can say is that God is very near to us in those tough times. True love is out there. You've just got to know where to look.

I want you know that your heavenly Dad will never love you and leave you. He always has your best interests at heart, and he's there for the long haul. He's concerned with every miniscule little detail of your life, and you can always run to him when life hurts. Trust me, at times it will.

My dad used to give me some pretty sound advice. And now I'm passing it on for you to read once you're old enough to understand. It's this: Never be too much of a man to cry . . . just be sure that you go to the right place.

I love you forever,

Dad

Love:
Know it and
Grow in it . . .

> 'Don't be afraid. I saved you. I named you. You are mine. When you have troubles, I am with you. When you cross rivers, you will not be hurt. When you walk through fire, you will not be burned; the flames will not hurt you. That's because I, the LORD, am your God. I, the Holy One of Israel, am your Saviour . . . You are precious to me, and I have given you a special place of honour. I love you.'

(Isaiah 43:1–4)

THERE ARE LOADS OF DIFFERENT TYPES OF LOVE. You can love your dog, your cat, your friends, your parents, your boyfriend/girlfriend . . . you can even love your mobile phone if you really want to, but they're all different types of love. For instance I'm guessing (or at least I'm hoping) you wouldn't love your mobile phone in the same way that you love your mum!

It says in the Bible that the greatest kind of love is the love of God. You see God's love is higher, wider, deeper, bigger and more satisfying than any other kind of love you will ever experience. I know that my mum loves me so much and she would do anything for me. It's really hard to think that God loves me even more than that but he totally does.

That's what's so amazing about it! There is nothing in the whole universe that will ever out-do God's love. He is the ultimate inventor of love, so no one can go one better than God.

I remember when I was at primary school, we always used to sing a song called 'He's Got the Whole World in His Hands'. You might have sung it too. We used to sing it at least once a week and I hated it because I thought it was a really boring song. It just repeated the same thing over and over again. But now, when I take a look at the words of that song, it talks about the truth. You see, God really has got the whole world in his hands and that world includes you and me.

Let me set a few things straight about God's love for you:

- When you do something wrong it does NOT mean that God is going to stop loving you. God's love for you is unconditional. That means that what you do doesn't change the amount of love he has for you. It will always stay the same, and there will always be loads of it. **GOD LOVES YOU NO MATTER WHAT.**

- God will NOT stop loving you because you forget to pray or read your Bible. God wants to be your friend. The only reason he sent his son, Jesus, to die on the cross was so that he could have a friendship with you. **HE WANTS TO BE YOUR FRIEND.**

- God does NOT just love people who are good-looking or talented. God created you and has just as much love for you as he does for everyone else. He doesn't look at your spots, or smell your stinky feet, or examine the shape of your bum. He looks at your heart and your personality. **GOD CREATED YOU.**

Check out these Bible verses about love:

Deuteronomy 6:5

1 Corinthians 13:4–7

You are God's prince/princess and he is totally crazy about you. Know it and grow in it!

Shell Perris, *Something to Shout About*, Authentic Media, 2006

ReactionReactionReactionReaction

CIRCLE:

😊 😞 😐 😯 😕 😲

TICK:

Total rubbish ☐ Not sure ☐ Worth thinking about ☐ Genius ☐

FILL:

....

....

....

....

Father knows best

When one of my children is leaving for a long time I feel anxiety and a more intense love for them, a protective love kicks in which isn't necessarily there for my kids whose circumstances are staying the same. I sometimes feel a really proud love when people say nice things about my children. Love can express itself in different ways but it is always there.

Discipline, Anyone?

Helen talks

When I was about eight years old I was desperate to learn how to play the piano; I just had to have lessons. I nagged and nagged my parents day in and day out for a piano and a teacher. They asked the expected parently questions, 'Do you realize you'll have to do a lot of practice?' and 'Will you keep going long term and not give up? Pianos are expensive, if we're going to buy one you need to make sure you go to all your lessons and do all your practice and stick at it.' Of course I agreed. I couldn't imagine not wanting to practise or wanting to give up. All I could think of was playing the piano.

S o finally the day came, a nice old wooden upright piano was installed upstairs at home, the required *Beginner Piano Book 1* was purchased and I had my first lesson. Things were going well. I learned my scales, I learned little rhymes to help me remember which of the black dots on the page were which note, I even learned a simple song to play (I think it only had one note in it, but at the time I thought it was Mozart). Anyway, things were going great and then it happened. **I STARTED TO GET BORED. IT STARTED TO GET DIFFICULT**. Suddenly I realized that in order to pull off the exercises and pieces in my lessons I really would have to practise every day, on my own, sitting at that boring piano in that boring upstairs room when it was sunny outside and I had new roller skates.

Well, unfortunately for me, my teacher and my parents, I just didn't have the discipline; I started skiving off, much to my parents' annoyance. They would try and make me practise and I would sit up at the piano and sulk and bang around on the keys and kick the piano and stuff. Understandably this would make my parents rather annoyed and they were firm believers in smacking! I know lots of people disagree with smacking now but my parents believed that there was nothing wrong with a smack with a slipper to help us kids remember what they were trying to teach us. Anyway, one day I had been particularly pushing my luck with the piano and was being really stroppy; my mum had had enough. To cut a long story short my mum ended up chasing me around the house trying to give me a smack, which I was running away from trying to avoid. Of course running away didn't really help matters because it just made her more angry!

I'm all grown up now and I must say that the discipline my parents gave me when I was a kid hasn't had any bad effects on me. I'm actually a fairly hard-working and self-motivated person now so I guess it seems to have worked. The Bible says in Hebrews 12:10, **'OUR FATHERS ON EARTH DISCIPLINED US FOR A SHORT TIME IN THE WAY THEY THOUGHT WAS BEST. BUT GOD DISCIPLINES US TO HELP US SO THAT WE CAN BE HOLY LIKE HIM.'** Sometimes we can think God doesn't love us if we don't get everything just the way we want it. We get annoyed if our prayers don't get answered the way we think they should, or when life gets hard and God seems far away. Sometimes this is just God disciplining us because he loves us. Sometimes it takes some tough love for us to learn a useful lesson from God that will make us more like him in the long run. Don't run away from God's discipline, embrace it as another facet of his love.

ReactionReactionReactionReaction

CIRCLE:

TICK:
Total rubbish ☐   Not sure ☐   Worth thinking about ☐   Genius ☐

FILL:

....

....

....

....

Reality Check

I LOVE YOU, DAD

Here's an opportunity for you to respond to God's love and show him just how much you appreciate him in return. You're going to write him a letter! Take time to think about what you really want to say before you write it, and we promise you'll get a lot more out of it that way. Also, if you want, you can write a similar letter to your earthly dad (or other father-figure in your life) on the back. You might find that there are a few similarities, and your dad will probably appreciate reading what you wrote to Father God as well.

TOP TIPS: Why not go the extra mile and put it in an envelope and everything? Or if snail mail doesn't work for you, why not email him instead? Only one rule, though – you can't put it off until Father's Day!

Father God,

I'm writing this as a simple 'thank you' for

....
....

I really respect and appreciate your

....
....

Your love for me enables me to

....
....

As your child, I want you to know that

....
....

I love you so much! How much? This much:

....
....

From

Date

Dad,

I'm writing this as a simple 'thank you' for

....
....
....
....

You are the perfect dad for me because

....
....
....
....

You help me understand God's love when you

....
....
....
....

As your child, I want you to know that

....
....
....
....

I love you so much! How much? This much:

....
....
....
....

      From

      Date

The Father's Power

The LORD All-Powerful said, 'Children honour their fathers. Servants honour their masters. I am your Father, so why don't you honour me? I am your master, so why don't you respect me?'

(Malachi 1:6)

2

First up

It's the age-old childhood argument . . .

'My dad is bigger than your dad.'

'Oh yeah? Well my dad is <u>stronger</u> than your dad.'

'<u>No way!</u> My dad could beat up your dad any day.'

'<u>Yeah right</u>. My dad would win blindfolded with one arm tied behind his back!'

. . . and on it goes. But do the two dads ever actually end up fighting? Probably not. Do the two kids end up fighting? Probably. After all, it was never really about whose <u>dad</u> was bigger anyway, was it?

Undoubtedly, our heavenly Dad truly is the biggest, strongest, most powerful father of all time – and we're not just saying that to pick a fight. The Bible describes God as the creator of everything that has ever existed, the one who sustains all that now exists, and the one who controls everything that will take place in the future. So basically all of eternity is in his capable hands. Nothing takes him by surprise or catches him off-guard. He is omnipotent. That means he is all-powerful.

In this next lesson, we're going to take a closer look at our heavenly Dad's unstoppable power. Our prayer is that as you read this and begin to understand just how strong our God is, you will find it easier to honour him, respect him and put your trust in him. That way, when the cares of this life try to 'pick a fight' with you, you'll be better equipped to respond with confidence, 'My Dad is *way* stronger than yours.'

CREATION

chipK's mind

A few years ago, Helen and I had the amazing opportunity of spending six weeks in New Zealand. Most of the time we were working, but shortly before we left we had about a week to check out some of the breathtaking scenery this island nation has to offer. One such stop off was at a place right next to the big mountain you'll see at the start of every Paramount film – it's called Fox Glacier. We felt like Arctic explorers as we slowly and carefully trekked up the icy glacier, stopping only to top up our water bottles with the freshest, cleanest, most freezing cold water we'd ever tasted from tiny babbling waterfalls along the way. We also went to Lake Mattheson where we took pictures from a spot called the 'Holy of Holies'. It was, undoubtedly, the single most beautiful landscape view I'd ever seen. When our photographs were developed, they simply paled in comparison to seeing the majesty of God's creation first-hand.

When God created the earth, he hid little clues about himself everywhere. The gentle beauty of an ocean sunset, the fury of a volcanic eruption, even the slow, steady flowing of a mighty ancient glacier . . . These are all characteristics of the Creator himself. It's up to us to discover them for ourselves.

God's mind

Yes, God has made it clear to them. There are things about God that people cannot see – his eternal power and all that makes him God. But since the beginning of the world, those things have been easy for people to understand. They are made clear in what God has made. So people have no excuse for the evil they do.

(Romans 1:19b–20)

The heavens tell about the glory of God. The skies announce what his hands have made. Each new day tells more of the story, and each night reveals more and more about God's power. You cannot hear them say anything. They don't make any sound we can hear. But their message goes throughout the world. Their teaching reaches the ends of the earth.

(Psalm 19:1–4)

> You lazy people, you should watch what the ants do and learn from them.

(Proverbs 6:6)

Your mind

- What is the most beautiful natural view/sight I've ever seen?
  ....
  ....

- Why did God take the time to 'hide' his characteristics in his creation instead of just telling plainly?
  ....
  ....

- What can I learn about God by studying these examples from nature?

  A tree:...

  A sunset:..

  An African lion:...

  A snowflake:...

  A mountain:...

  A waterfall:...

  A slug:..

- I will take time to stop and consider God's attributes in his creation by:
  ....
  ....

Chip Kendall, *The Mind of chipK: Enter at Your Own Risk*, Authentic Media, 2006

ReactionReactionReactionReaction

CIRCLE:

☺ ☹ 😐 😲 🙂 😮

TICK:

Total rubbish ☐ Not sure ☐ Worth thinking about ☐ Genius ☐

FILL:

....

....

....

....

Father knows best

God's power is inextricably linked to his love. He has the power to crush but he chooses not to. Knowing he has that power and he chooses not to use it draws us closer to him. His love will always cause him to do the best thing for us.

With GREAT POWER...

Ben talks

In the comic book and film versions of the Spider-Man original story, a character speaks the classic line:

'With great power comes great responsibility.'

This sentence is of great significance in the context of Spider-Man's story. Here is a young man, who is suddenly gifted with unbelievable power. Used well, this power will see Spider-Man become the hero of the story. Used selfishly, on the other hand, he could end up no better than the villains he is supposed to be fighting.

Did you know that this line actually comes from the Bible? In Luke's Gospel, Jesus tells his disciples that to those who are given much, much is expected.

This can be applied to so many areas of our lives, from our talents and gifts, to the physical comforts and treasures we accumulate. First and foremost, though, this applies to the power that we receive from God.

There is none more powerful than God! Unlike the villains in comic books, God is not a power maniac. He will never abuse his power. The good news is that God uses his strength to save, and then empowers us to live life to the full for him. We get all our strength and power from him, and he expects us to put it to good use! Just as the city of New York calls on Spider-Man to use his great power to serve and help the people in those stories, so Father God calls and authorizes us to use the power he gives us to love and help each other in the real world.

Read Luke 12:48. See also Jeremiah 10:12, 2 Corinthians 13:4, Ephesians 6:10.

Reflect

- *In what ways has God demonstrated his power throughout the Bible?*
- *How can you grow in your own trust of God's power and authority, and reveal this to the world around you?*

Respond

Pray this prayer every morning this week before you get out of bed:

'Father God, thank you for your saving power. Help me to live in your strength today. Empower me to love as you love so that the world will learn to trust in your unfailing love and power. Amen'

Remember

God is completely powerful and trustworthy. He will empower you to see this world impacted with his love. What will you do with what he gives you?

ReactionReactionReactionReaction

CIRCLE:

TICK:

Total rubbish ☐   Not sure ☐   Worth thinking about ☐   Genius ☐

FILL:

....

....

....

I PREDICT AN EARTHQUAKE...

Helen talks

Chip and I went to college in a town just outside LA in California, USA (not just saying that to make you jealous, it is relevant!). Any of you who have studied geography will know that LA sits on top of a massive fault line and is therefore prone to earthquakes.

Coming from the UK, which is basically the safest place in the world (think about it: no tornadoes, no massive tidal waves, no poisonous snakes/spiders, no crocodiles, no earthquakes), I was a little freaked out by the whole earthquake thing. My roommate went to a seminar about earthquakes and then decided to get prepared. We bought their $10 'earthquake survival kits' (basically some plasters, food bars and a silver blanket) and we started practising for earthquakes. We would try to hold onto our earthquake kits while jumping off our beds and climbing around the place. Probably not the best preparation but we had fun!

There have always been predictions that 'the big one' will one day hit Southern California but despite this it is one of the most densely populated and expensive areas of the USA. It's easy to see why. It's a great place – summer all year round, beautiful mountains and beaches, nice enough to make you want to take the risk – but **AT ANY MOMENT EVERYTHING COULD CHANGE DRAMATICALLY.**

In some ways God's power is similar. We love to live in God's grace, to dance in the sunshine of his love and acceptance but we don't often think about his judgement. We like to skip over those parts in the Bible where God wipes whole towns or people groups off the face of the earth, or strikes individuals dead because of their lies or disobedience (read the story in Acts 5). Ultimately God is more powerful than we can possibly imagine and we need to live with a healthy respect for that power and make sure we don't take advantage of his grace. The Bible says in Proverbs 9:10, 'Wisdom begins with fear and respect for the LORD. Knowledge of the Holy One leads to understanding'.

Read Hebrews 12:18–29 and write down some of the characteristics of God mentioned in this passage.

Father knows best

As a parent of a young child you have responsibility and power to influence, but as your children get older you find you have responsibility without power. When they are younger you do have power. You stop them crossing the road, etc. As they get older and start to make their own decisions you choose to release the power you have over them. Maintaining responsibility while reducing your power over them . . . that's a hard one to live with.

Name: **Bonny Cleasby**
Age: **17 yrs**
Town: **Oxford**

Passions: **Most things, anything that grips my attention.**

What are you not passionate about?

Rap/hip hop/RnB

Peanut butter or marmite?

They taste really good together, but if I had to choose one – marmite.

Who do you really respect?

C.S. Lewis. I'm a huge fan.

How do you know when your dad is mad at you?

When his voice goes 10 octaves lower.

What is the worst punishment you've ever had from your dad?

Banning me from music – I cried.

What's the nicest thing your dad has ever done?

When I was born he sold his boat to look after us.

Getaway Car - God's Power to Forgive

Helen talks

Have you ever had that sinking feeling in the pit of your stomach where you know you have messed up? It's the worst. Slowly it dawns on you that you've just been caught out for doing something you knew wasn't right but were sure you'd get away with. It feels like someone has just dropped a stone in your stomach and you just want to disappear. All those questions start going through your mind – 'Why couldn't I have just waited?' or 'Why didn't I do it like this?' or 'If I'd just done . . . could I have got away with it?' But you know deep down, like it or not, you are busted! It's at that point that you want someone to come speeding up in a very fast car (like in the movies), shout, 'Jump in!' and then drive away at 100 mph to somewhere where they can't get you.

O f course in real life you know it's not going to happen, no one is going to get you out of it and **YOU ARE GOING TO HAVE TO PAY THE PRICE FOR WHAT YOU'VE DONE**. Most of the time it's a good thing that justice is done and you have to pay for the wrong things you do – it should help you stop doing it again! However, imagine something even worse. Imagine you've done something so bad that you deserve the death penalty! There are countries in the world where, for relatively small offences, you can be sentenced to death. Imagine what your stomach would feel like then. No second chances, no opportunity to do your time and make up for it, the end, finished.

In God's eyes sin has just this effect. Because God is holy and just, he can't stand sin, even the smallest bit of wrongdoing ultimately deserves death in his eyes. Does that seem unreasonable? To our human minds maybe it does, but God is a perfect judge and perfect in holiness so it is impossible for us to live up to his standards. But here is the good news – the guy in the fast car. God is so powerful and loving that he created a way for us to be forgiven – a fast car for us to escape from sin and death in.

The Bible says, 'God gave Jesus as a way to forgive people's sins through their faith in him. God can forgive them because the blood sacrifice of Jesus pays for their sins. God gave Jesus to show that he always does what is right and fair. He was right in the past when he was patient and did not punish people for their sins' (Romans 3:25). God knew that we would sin and that ultimately that would mean death. He also knew that he wanted to have a relationship with mankind which he could not do if sin was in the way. So God became man, he came to earth to die as Jesus, a perfect man, 100% human and 100% God. **GOD PROVIDES THE FAST CAR AND SAYS, COME AWAY WITH ME**, you can be forgiven and live in relationship with me if you believe in Jesus and accept him as the only one who could save you from death.

John 3:16 says, 'This is how God showed his great love for the world: he gave his only Son, so that everyone who believes in him would not be lost but have eternal life.' We must never forget that it was God the Father who sent his one and only Son. He's the one that made the call and sent Jesus to rescue us. He deserves our respect. Tougher than the toughest Mafia boss and with more authority than any president or prime minister, your heavenly Dad chooses to send that getaway car to drive you as far away from your sins as the east is from the west.

ReactionReactionReactionReaction

CIRCLE:

TICK:

Total rubbish ☐   Not sure ☐   Worth thinking about ☐   Genius ☐

FILL:

....

....

....

....

Father knows best

When the child is very young and it hasn't got the health and safety warnings built into its head, you exercise absolute power. If it is running out into the road you grab it and restrain it. Then there are later stages when you use your power to provide examples and opportunities and then release them to make their own decisions.

Knowledge is power. When your children are young they trust you to operate power. But it's a wonderful, rewarding power when your children get older and ask you for advice or wisdom or direction and you think, 'Wow, they want to hear something from me'.

Dear Rob,

This morning as I was waking up, I had an overwhelming urge to write to you about something you're bound to ask yourself sooner or later. If God is so strong and good, then why didn't he heal my dad?

You have no idea of the range of emotions this thought brings to the surface for me. The last thing that I'd ever want my condition to produce in you is any doubt in God's supernatural power. Even a tiny one. I still believe 100% that God can heal me if he wants to, and I'll continue to trust him until the day I die. My faith in God is what gives me hope that you and your mother will go on to experience true joy in life, even if he chooses to take me home to heaven in this way. I've made my peace with God, and I can honestly say — just like the three young Hebrew men facing certain death in Daniel 3:17–18, 'If you throw us into the hot furnace, the God we serve can save us. And if he wants to, he can save us from your power. But even if God does not save us, we want you to know, King, that we refuse to serve your gods. We will not worship the gold idol you have set up.'

There's something strangely triumphant about keeping faith in God against all the odds. Maybe it's because it so displeases the devil. It completely disarms him and gives him no leg to stand on. Just as love conquers fear, I believe that trust conquers doubt. And that makes the devil both a liar and a loser.

I don't know how much longer I have left to live. Each new day really is a gift from heaven. But I do know that God is God and I am not. His ways are higher than mine and he knows exactly what he's doing. My prayer is that both in life and death, I might be an example for you to follow as someone who trusted in God no matter what.

I love you forever,

Dad

LET GO.
Let God.

Ben talks

The Lord of the Rings had always been high on my list of books to read at some point in my life. They are pretty mega-sized books and so, truth be told, when the films came out I was glad to have a way of enjoying the story without having to give up my social life for 3 years (I'm a slow reader).

One of the key characters in the story is a creature called Gollum. As the heroes embark on an epic quest to rid their land of a darkly magical ring, Gollum becomes increasingly important to the story. You see, Gollum was the keeper of the ring at one stage, and is now consumed by the power of it. All he can think about is getting it back. We learn that Gollum was an ordinary hobbit at one time, who has now been completely physically and mentally changed by his coveting of the powerful ring. By the end of the story, Gollum's fate is sealed when he is unable to let go of his desire for the ring, and it becomes the death of him.

God is asking us to trust and surrender our lives to him. Sometimes that involves letting go of things that are harmful for us, or that get in the way of his purposes for our lives. **GOD IS BIG ENOUGH TO KNOW WHAT'S BEST FOR US AND STRONG ENOUGH TO HELP US LET GO OF THE THINGS THAT AREN'T.**

Read Mark 10:17–22. See also Jeremiah 29:11, Psalm 18:1–3, Romans 15:13.

Reflect

- *What can we learn from the story of the rich young man in Mark's Gospel?*
- *Is there something in your life that you know God is calling you to let go of so that you can move forward with him?*

Respond

Partner with a friend in exploring whether God might be calling you to let go of something. Commit to praying about it together regularly, encourage and challenge each other as you submit to God's will for your life.

Remember

God knows what is best for us, and is strong enough to help us let go of anything in our lives that isn't.

ReactionReactionReactionReaction

CIRCLE:

TICK:

Total rubbish ☐   Not sure ☐   Worth thinking about ☐   Genius ☐

FILL:

....
....
....
....

HEALING

chipK's mind

Some people think that miraculous healings only happened back in Bible times. Hogwash! How do I know? Because I've experienced one myself.

When I was a kid, my left foot was turned in slightly. It affected the way I stood, walked, ran – everything. One night my dad sensed God's leading to pray for my foot to be healed as he tucked me into bed. I was already asleep, but as he prayed for me, my foot turned straight, and by the **NEXT MORNING IT WAS OBVIOUS THAT I'D BEEN COMPLETELY HEALED**. After that, I was always the fastest runner in my class at school, and I ended up going to a Performing Arts Academy after I graduated. I think it's safe to say that had it not been for that miraculous experience, I'd not be the on-stage dancing, mental lunatic that I am today.

This is just one of many stories of people being physically healed all over the world in our time. There are other types of healing too. Some people experience emotional healing from past hurts and abuse. Others may need healing in their minds.

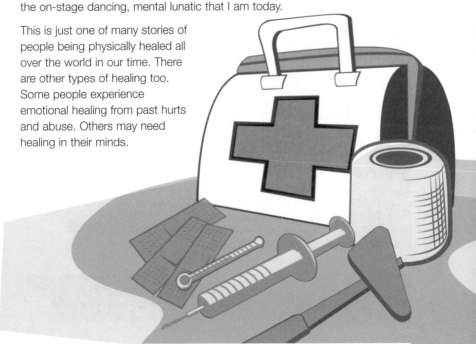

Everyone who becomes a follower of Jesus experiences a sort of 'spiritual' healing to some degree. We've gone from being children trapped in darkness, stuck in a prison of doing what's wrong, to being children of 'light', set free to enjoy the pleasures of God forever.

Not all supernatural healings happen instantly. Sometimes God chooses to heal us over a period of time. In some cases, God chooses to not heal people at all (not in the way they expect him to anyway). In times like these, no matter how stubborn we may be, we have to trust that he knows what he's doing. After all, he is God isn't he!

God's mind

But he was being punished for what we did. He was crushed because of our guilt. He took the punishment we deserved, and this brought us peace. We were healed because of his pain.
(Isaiah 53:5)

When Jesus heard this, he said to them, 'Sick people are the ones who need a doctor, not those who are healthy. I came to ask sinners to join me, not those who do everything right.'
(Mark 2:17)

When the sun went down, the people brought their sick friends to Jesus. They had many different kinds of sicknesses. Jesus laid his hands on each sick person and healed them all.
(Luke 4:40)

'The Son of Man has power on earth to forgive sins. But how can I prove this to you? Maybe you are thinking it was easy for me to say to the paralysed man, "Your sins are forgiven," because there's no proof it really happened. But what if I say to the man, "Stand up. Take your mat and walk"? Then you will be able to see if I really have this power or not.' So Jesus said to the paralysed man, 'I tell you, stand up. Take your mat and go home.' The paralysed man stood up. He picked up his mat and went straight out of the door with everyone watching. They were amazed and praised God. They said, 'This is the most amazing thing we have ever seen!'
(Mark 2:9–12)

Are you sick? Ask the elders of the church to come and put oil on you in the name of the Lord and pray for you. If such a prayer is offered in faith, it will heal anyone who is sick.

The Lord will heal them. And if they have sinned, he will forgive them.

(James 5:14–15)

'Then, if my people who are called by my name become humble and pray, and look to me for help, and turn away from their evil ways, I will hear them from heaven. I will forgive their sin and heal their land.'

(2 Chronicles 7:14)

Your mind

Is there something I'd like to be healed from:

- **Physically? (in my body)**

  ....

- **Mentally? (in my mind)**

  ....

- **Emotionally? (in my feelings)**

  ....

- **Spiritually? (in my heart)**

  ....

Who can I talk to that will pray with me to find healing?

Who can I pray for right now to receive healing?

When it comes to healing, why is it always better to pray in groups of two or more? (HINT: Read Matthew 18:19–20)

Chip Kendall, *The Mind of chipK: Enter at Your Own Risk*, Authentic Media, 2006

ReactionReactionReactionReaction

CIRCLE:

☺ ☹ 😐 😮 😕 😲

TICK:

Total rubbish ☐   Not sure ☐   Worth thinking about ☐   Genius ☐

FILL:

....

....

....

....

Father knows best

One of my underlying philosophies has been to let my children discover things and then make their own choices. What you learn for yourself will count for the rest of your life. I tried not to ram things down their throats, but to lead by example and then provide an environment where my children can learn and experience first hand and then make their own choices.

FEAR GOD

chipK's mind

Nobody likes to be sent to the principal's office – unless, of course, you are receiving some sort of award. Nobody likes getting all dressed up for weddings – unless of course, you're a girl. Nobody likes standing before a judge in a court of law – unless, of course, you've just been proven innocent.

So why do we do all these things anyway? Out of reverence and respect, that's why. The principal has the authority to kick you out of school, if he chooses. That bride and groom are about to promise the rest of their lives to each other. That judge has enough credentials to put you in the slammer for life.

Sadly some people misunderstand the phrase, 'The fear of the Lord'. They think it means that you should be afraid of God, as if he's about to strike you with lightning or something terrible like that. This couldn't be further from the truth. Fearing God simply means showing respect where it's due. Give honour to your Creator Father who holds the universe in the palm of his powerful yet gentle hand. Have a bit of reverence for him next time you set foot into his presence, but don't be afraid. After all, the cross of Jesus has already proved your innocence.

God's mind

Knowledge begins with fear and respect for the LORD, but stubborn fools hate wisdom and refuse to learn.
(Proverbs 1:7)

Wisdom teaches you to respect the LORD. You must be humbled before you can be honoured.
(Proverbs 15:33)

Remember your Creator while you are young, before the bad times come – before the years come when you say, 'I have wasted my life' ... The most important thing a person can do is to respect God and obey his commands.
(Ecclesiastes 12:1,13)

Your mind

- **Who else do I show respect for (besides God)?**

  ....

  ....

- **When do I find that I'm afraid of God? Why is this?**

  ....

  ....

- **How do I practically show my respect for God?**

  ....

  ....

- **Which of these positions demonstrate reverence?**

Sitting – Standing – Kneeling

Lying on back – Lying on front

Crouching – Slouching – Kneeling on one leg

Arms raised – Head lowered – Arms folded – Head stand

Chip Kendall,
The Mind of chipK: Enter at Your Own Risk,
Authentic Media, 2006

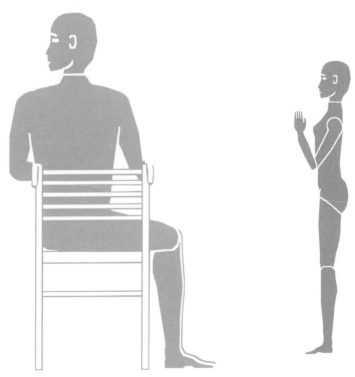

ReactionReactionReactionReaction

CIRCLE:

TICK:

Total rubbish ☐   Not sure ☐   Worth thinking about ☐   Genius ☐

FILL:

....

....

....

....

The Father's Grace

We pray that the Lord Jesus Christ himself and God our Father will comfort you and strengthen you in every good thing you do and say. God loved us and gave us through his grace a wonderful hope and comfort that has no end.

(2 Thessalonians 2:16,17)

First up

OK so we've looked a little deeper at our heavenly Father's unconditional love and his infinite power. Now it's time to move on to his grace. This is a massive topic, and there's absolutely no way we'll be able to cover every single aspect of it in this brief Life Lesson, but we do hope we can help kick-start a passion in your soul for understanding God's amazing, undeserved grace.

Have you ever done something you knew you were not supposed to do, and your friend willingly took the blame for your actions? That's grace. Have you ever lied to your mum, and she forgave you even though she knew you were lying? That's grace. Have you ever really tried to get your head around why Jesus had to die on the cross? John 3:16 says: 'This is how God showed his great love for the world: he gave his only Son, so that everyone who believes in him would not be lost but have eternal life.' Now *that* is grace.

Grace is when you get something you know you don't deserve. And our Dad in heaven has a ton of it. He has to! Just take a look at how much we as humans take him for granted. We disobey him and give him a bad name every single day of our lives – even Christians. And yet, the Bible says that while we were still sinners, Christ came (sent by the Father) and died for us. Just imagine, he actually cared about us enough to make that big a sacrifice even though we don't deserve it at all.

As you work your way through the excerpts that follow, try to think about the areas in your own life that require God's limitless grace on an ongoing basis. Surrender them to your heavenly Father and watch as he makes you more like Jesus. Before long, you may find that you actually enjoy some of the Christian disciplines you used to dread. Stuff like reading the Bible, worshipping and regularly spending time with God. All these things (and more!) become increasingly natural once you receive a real revelation of God's grace. Remember, as a Christian you don't have to be a slave any more . . . you are a child of the King.

> The Spirit that we received is not a spirit that makes us slaves again and causes us to fear. The Spirit that we have makes us God's chosen children. And with that Spirit we cry out, '*Abba*, Father'.

(Romans 8:15)

FIRST CLASS

Helen talks

A few years ago I was flying from London to LA to visit Chip. As I was standing in the queue for check-in, one of the airline staff came up to me. He said that they thought the plane might have been overbooked and they were looking for volunteers to wait and take a flight the following morning. I wasn't in a massive hurry, so I said OK. They sent me off to a café and told me to come back half an hour before the flight departed to check whether I could fly or if I had to wait.

When I came back they said they had managed to squeeze me onto the flight so they handed me a boarding card and told me to run! With just 25 minutes to spare I started my dash to the plane. I sweated nervously through the long queue in security, glancing at the time every few minutes, and then dashed for the gate. It was only once I got into the tunnel to the plane that I looked at my boarding card . . . Seat 4A.

'HMM THAT'S VERY CLOSE TO THE FRONT,' I THOUGHT. 'UPGRADE!'

I got on the plane and was ushered to my very enormous, very comfortable seat. I sat down looking a bit scruffy and dishevelled and feeling like I didn't fit in, but despite that, the stewardess welcomed me and handed me a drink. I got treated just the same as all the businessmen and rich people sitting with me in first class.

It was a great flight! Nice food with an actual metal knife and fork, plenty of leg room, a great entertainment system, and as much chocolate, nuts or anything else I fancied, whenever I wanted. No waiting for hours while hundreds of other people are served or until you reach cruising altitude or whatever.

Every once in a while I couldn't help glancing back into economy at all the people squished into their tiny seats, eating their nasty food from little metal containers, screaming children, people being sick – you know what it's like! Basically that was what I deserved; that was what I had paid for, just the same as everyone else back there. The difference was that I'd been shown grace by the airline and allowed something more. A big 'YES, you are allowed' had been written on my boarding card, instead of a big 'NO, get back in the cheap seats'.

I didn't really deserve my first class seat. I hadn't paid for it. This is like a little mini picture of God's grace to us. **GRACE IS FAVOUR THAT WE DON'T DESERVE AND HAVE DONE NOTHING TO EARN.** Romans 5:8 says, 'Christ died for us while we were still sinners, and by this God showed how much he loves us.' That is grace. While we were still living our own way with a big 'NO' attached to our lives, God sent his Son to pay our way into heaven. All we have to do is accept it.

- *Read through Romans 5 and see how many times the word 'grace' is used.*

- *Write down your own explanation of God's grace to us, in your own words.*

ReactionReactionReactionReaction

CIRCLE:

TICK:

Total rubbish ☐   Not sure ☐   Worth thinking about ☐   Genius ☐

FILL:

....

....

....

....

WHAT'S THE CATCH?

Ben talks

Have you ever been offered something for free, something that perhaps seemed too good to be true?

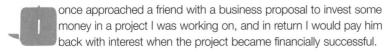

I once approached a friend with a business proposal to invest some money in a project I was working on, and in return I would pay him back with interest when the project became financially successful.

After a few days of thinking over the proposal, my friend called me and told me his decision. He was going to give me the money. Fantastic! I thought. However, before I could reassure him that it wouldn't be long before he would get his investment back, he said, 'Ben, I don't want anything back, this is a gift. **I'M NOT INVESTING IN YOUR BUSINESS, I'M INVESTING IN YOU.**'

I was gobsmacked; this was not a small amount of money. I couldn't help but think there would be some kind of catch somewhere. I was waiting for the terms and conditions, the list of requirements that would be needed to get the money. I could see myself needing to mow his lawn every weekend, or having to text him a joke every day for the next ten years! There must be some kind of condition attached to the gift, I thought, but the condition never came.

I had never considered having the investment without any strings attached. I couldn't for the life of me think what I had done to deserve such a generous gift. In reality, though, the gift said more about my friend than it did about me. This was a gift of love, given without requiring repayment, given because he wanted to.

What does the Bible say about God's gift of grace and what we have done to deserve it in the verses below?

The mistake we can make is thinking that we have done something to earn God's gift of grace. The truth is we haven't. His grace is given freely, simply because he wants to give it, even to those who would throw it back in his face. There will, of course, be a response by anyone who truly recognizes that grace, and it is in this response of faith that we can know him more fully, be transformed by him, and have joy in the eternal life that follows.

Read Ephesians 2:4–9. See also John 1:14–17, Romans 3:20–24, Hebrews 4:16.

Reflect

- *How might recognizing God's gift of grace bring about changes in the way you live your life?*
- *In what ways could you reflect the grace you have received from God to the world you live in?*

Respond

Be generous with your time, talents and possessions. Be quick to forgive those who do you wrong and show kindness to those you struggle with, and see how people respond to this reflection of God's own grace.

Remember

God's grace is a gift, given to us because he wants to give it. We cannot earn it, and we certainly do not deserve it. Truly recognizing this gift should change how we live our lives.

ReactionReactionReactionReaction

CIRCLE:

TICK:

Total rubbish ☐   Not sure ☐   Worth thinking about ☐   Genius ☐

FILL:

....

....

....

....

....

....

The following is taken from the end of a book (a true story) about a woman's search for her birth father. We've included it here because we think it paints such a beautiful picture of God's heart towards his children. By this point in the story, she and her husband Tim have finally tracked down her father Theo in Cyprus . . .

DANCING FATHER

There were few communication barriers between my father and me. He spoke better English than my cousin Antonios. They wanted to take us to a restaurant with real Greek food and music. While Tim spoke to Antonios, I walked arm in arm with my father. We were joined together in victory as father and daughter, parent and child. I told him that I knew we would be so alike, and we were. Everything I was feeling, he was speaking out. For every time I thought, *Thank you God*, my father spoke it into the warm and inviting evening air of Larnaca. When I stopped to reflect on how beautiful he was, he would tell me how beautiful I was to him. He put into words the beatings of my heart.

Tim contacted people in England, telling everyone how he was about to have dinner with his father-in-law. His phone did not stop ringing with voices of our stunned friends. In the restaurant I made sure that I sat next to Theo. I looked at Tim to make sure he was fine. The expression of amazement never once left his face. Theo touched very little on his plate, and I had just enough to soak up the wine! **IT WAS JUST SO WONDERFUL SITTING IN A GREEK RESTAURANT WITH MY DAD.** I had dreamt of this since sitting in such a restaurant as a teenager, convinced that Mum was about to tell me about my father . . . But now I was here at the end, and it was so perfect. What I had longed for over Christmas had been a shallow undercoat of the vibrancy and colour of this reunion.

Theo looked at me and announced without embarrassment, 'Right, I am going to dance for you now.' He rose from the table and danced without shame to the staccato rhythm of the traditional Greek music. As the restaurant looked on, I felt God say, 'You have danced for your father for so long, now it is time for him to dance for you.'

I had to pinch myself. God had turned my father's heart towards me in a reunion beyond anything I had been capable of dreaming of. Theo called me over and we danced together. I don't think that I have ever smiled so much in my life.

Amanda Lord and Simon Lord, *Search for a Father*, **Authentic Media, 2006**

ReactionReactionReactionReaction

CIRCLE:

TICK:

Total rubbish ☐   Not sure ☐   Worth thinking about ☐   Genius ☐

FILL:

....

....

....

....

Let's Talk

I had just got back from two months in South America on mission and I was tired. Lying on my bed I was enjoying the opportunity to simply chat to God; it felt like the first time in ages that we'd had the chance to catch up and ask each other, 'How you doing?'

T his prayer session took me to a place of God's presence that I don't think I'd ever been to before. I was right there in the 'sanctuary' talking to God, my Dad, about all the stupid things that swim around in my head. It was two weeks before the start of my final year at university, so my main focus was the future. **'WHERE AM I GOING, DADDY? WHAT HAVE YOU GOT PLANNED FOR ME?** My husband, Daddy, how's he doing today? Do I know him yet? What about my kids, are you looking after them for me? Will you look after them when I mess up or let them down?' I started thinking about being pregnant with those kids I was praying for – me with a big belly and stretch marks. 'O God! Am I going to have swollen ankles when I'm pregnant?'

I was in the throne room of the Holy God Most High and all I could hear was laughter ringing in my ears. I had the most direct access to the Author and Perfector of everything, able to ask him anything – and the question in my head was not about world poverty or the mystery of the Trinity, but whether I am going to get swollen ankles when I'm pregnant! The delight I could feel from God because of that question still makes me giggle today.

Prayer is not about the right phrases or how many Bible quotes you can include. It's about sitting down with Daddy and catching up with him. He wants you. **HE WANTS YOU TO SIT ON HIS KNEE.** From there you can share your heart with him and capture his heart for you. From there comes the inspiration to live a life that honours Daddy. You know him, you know what it takes to make him proud. But you also know that when you don't cut it, when you don't make the grade – all he wants is for you to come and sit back on his knee so he can wipe away the tears, give you a hug and whisper in your ear, 'I love you. I love you. I love you.'

I look at those around me, and I see that so many have no concept of someone whispering 'I love you' in their ears. Somewhere in our lives we get broken. We all have a moment when we were told we were never going to be good enough. That we are not going to make the grade. We live our lives in the knowledge that we have failed to live up to expectations, we suffer guilt knowing that we've let someone down.

Part of our communication with God is about allowing him to heal that wound, allowing him to show us that he didn't make a mistake when he made us, that he loves us just as we are. He wants us to have the right relationship with him as our Father, our heavenly Father. A relationship where the things we have longed for in our relationships are fulfilled in him. I know many people who struggle with the fatherhood of God. I know I did. But I do have a perfect image of what I wanted from my dad, even if I don't necessarily get it. I know what the relationship could have looked like. And I know that God offers me exactly that picture.

Andy Frost and Jo Wells,
Freestyle,
Authentic Media, 2005

CIRCLE:

☺ ☹ 😐 😤 😌 😲

TICK:

Total rubbish ☐   Not sure ☐   Worth thinking about ☐   Genius ☐

FILL:

....

....

....

....

Father knows best

The Bible says that fathers shouldn't provoke their children, and it's not difficult to provoke them! So the gracious bit is to recognize that they are children, they aren't mature. If you are unreasonable with them they will respond disproportionately and that's not helpful. Showing grace helps maintain relationships rather than destroy them.

Pay it Forward >>>

Chip talks

Cheryl was very stressed. She'd promised her dad that she would pay back the £500 he'd loaned her by Friday. It was now Thursday night, and after saving all her babysitting money and tips from work, she'd only managed to scrape £320 together. Cheryl knew that her dad was a real stickler for keeping promises. How was she going to confront him? What would he say?

Friday night, as the whole family sat down to dinner, Cheryl's dad looked over at her, and without him having to say a word, she knew what he was thinking. This was the moment of truth that she'd been dreading for the past 24 hours.

'Dad,' she began, putting her fork down, **'I'm really sorry, but I can't pay you back the full £500 you loaned me. I know I promised I'd get it to you today, but all I've got is £320.'**

Her dad paused a moment before replying. It felt like an eternity. Finally he looked up at Cheryl and a big smile spread across his face.

'It's OK,' he said. **'You don't need to pay me back the rest.'**

Cheryl was shocked, but she felt as though a massive burden had been lifted from her shoulders. But before she could open her mouth to thank him, he continued.

'In fact,' he said, **'you don't even need to pay me the money you've got saved. Just promise me that you'll "pay it forward".'**

'Pay it forward'? What in the world was that supposed to mean? Cheryl's dad went on to explain that the best way for her to respond to his generosity was if she were to act generously herself in some way. By giving that £320 to someone who really needed it, Cheryl would be bringing the same relief she felt to someone else. And if they in turn responded in some other significant way by paying it forward, then the knock-on effect of that first act of grace by Cheryl's dad could be truly transformational.

Just like Cheryl's dad, our Father in heaven has lavished his grace upon us in so many ways. As disciples of Jesus, shouldn't we respond by paying it forward?

Read the story of the three servants in Matthew 25:14–30.

- *What were the consequences for the servants who wisely invested their money?*

Now read the story of the unmerciful servant in Matthew 18:21–35.

- *What was the consequence for the servant who didn't show the same grace he'd been shown?*

- *How is the story of the lost son (Luke 15:11–32) similar to the story above, and how is it a picture of our heavenly Father's grace towards us when we turn back to him?*

ReactionReactionReactionReaction

CIRCLE:

☺ ☹ 😐 😮 😕 😲

TICK:

Total rubbish ☐   Not sure ☐   Worth thinking about ☐   Genius ☐

FILL:

....

....

Father knows best

As a father, what cheers me up more than anything is when my children choose to talk to me. That's the nature of God inside us. Psychologists say that the greatest need of man is to walk into a room and find someone happy to see us. God designed us to be happy in fellowship with him.

chipK's mind

No doubt about it, the Chinese are amazing athletes. Need proof? Check 'em out at the Olympic Games. They have an unbelievable knack of combining strength, speed and beauty with an almost effortless flair.

ATHENS, GREECE, 2004

THE FINALS COMPETITION FOR MEN'S SYNCHRONIZED DIVING

China was ranked number one by the end of the heats, and all they needed was one more of those famous performances to clinch the gold. Just one dive left. And then . . . belly-flop. The judges' scores all came up – zero. Those two Chinese divers had gone from hero status to zero status and all in a matter of seconds.

The Bible encourages us to run the race with perseverance, comparing our lives to a competition, just like in the Olympics. But I can't help thinking that, actually, if we're really honest with ourselves, we can identify more with those two unfortunate Chinese guys than any of the hundreds of gold medallists. We belly-flop every day when we mess up and sin, yet we're still encouraged to press on towards the prize of heaven. God's grace says, 'You know what? **EVEN THOUGH YOU'VE BELLY-FLOPPED, I'VE STILL GOT A GOLD MEDAL WITH YOUR NAME ON IT.'** That's something we need to hear loud and clear . . . and not just every four years.

God's mind

We have all these great people around us as examples. Their lives tell us what faith means. So we, too, should run the race that is before us and never give up. We should remove from our lives anything that would slow us down and the sin that so often makes us fall. We must never stop looking to Jesus. He is the leader of our faith, and he is the one who makes our faith complete. He suffered death on a cross. But he accepted the shame of the cross as if it were nothing because of the joy he could see waiting for him. And now he is sitting at the right side of God's throne. Think about Jesus. He patiently endured the angry insults that sinful people were shouting at him. Think about him so that you won't get discouraged and stop trying.

(Hebrews 12:1–3)

But the Lord said, 'My grace is all you need.'

(2 Corinthians 12:9a)

I don't mean that I am exactly what God wants me to be. I have not yet reached that goal. But I continue trying to reach it and make it mine. That's what Christ Jesus wants me to do. It is the reason he made me his. Brothers and sisters, I know that I still have a long way to go. But there is one thing I do: I forget what is in the past and try as hard as I can to reach the goal before me. I keep running hard towards the finish line to get the prize that is mine because God has called me through Christ Jesus to life up there in heaven.

(Philippians 3:12–14)

Athletes in a race must obey all the rules to win.

(2 Timothy 2:5)

Your mind

- **What do athletes spend most of their time doing?**

  ....
  ....

- **How does this apply to my personal 'Grace Olympics'?**

  ....
  ....

- **What is a simple definition of 'grace'? (HINT: Feel free to use a dictionary)**

  ....
  ....

- **What potential 'belly-flops' can I avoid today?**

  ....
  ....

ReactionReactionReactionReaction

CIRCLE:

TICK:

Total rubbish ☐   Not sure ☐   Worth thinking about ☐   Genius ☐

FILL:

....
....
....

CHIP: Whoa! Hold up a second. I'm not sure we should include this next excerpt.

HELEN: Why not?

CHIP: It starts off all right, but it gets into some deep stuff and a few of the words are pretty big ones.

HELEN: Are you telling me that you believe our readers are either way too young or way too thick for some of this material?

CHIP: No!

HELEN: Then what are you trying to say?

CHIP: Well, I don't know really.

HELEN: (sighs and rolls her eyes) Boys!

CHIP: (sighs and rolls his eyes, sarcastically) Girls!

HELEN: I tell you what, why don't we just go ahead and include the excerpt and let our readers decide for themselves if it's 'too deep' for them.

CHIP: OK. Fine. It's a deal. But they can't say I didn't at least *try* and warn them . . .

JOHN THE BAPTIZER

Everyone was hoping for the Messiah to come, and they wondered about John. They thought, 'Maybe he is the Messiah.' John's answer to this was, 'I baptize you with water, but there is someone coming later who is able to do more than I can. I am not good enough to be the slave who unties his sandals. He will baptize you with the Holy Spirit and with fire. He will come ready to clean the grain. He will separate the good grain from the chaff, and he will put the good part into his barn. Then he will burn the useless part with a fire that cannot be stopped.' John said many other things like this to encourage the people to change, and he told them the Good News. John criticized Herod the ruler for what he had done with Herodias, the wife of Herod's brother, as well as for all the other bad things he had done. So Herod added another bad thing to all his other wrongs: he put John in jail.

(Luke 3:15–20)

While my heart cherishes grace, my pride suppresses a grateful sigh of relief that should accompany undeserved forgiveness and coaxes me to earn God's favour. **MY SIN TUGS AT MY SHIRT, SUGGESTING THAT MORE GOOD DEEDS WILL APPEASE GOD'S SENSE OF JUSTICE.** So I say my prayers of obligation, and I count my righteous acts, anything to hear my coins clang into the collection box for the purchase of indulgences. My pride drinks deeply of the works-righteousness elixir, and I reject the pangs of humility that inevitably accompany a plea for mercy.

The Bible introduces John, unlike heroes such as David or Peter, without mentioning a single character flaw. We know John only as an obedient prophet, uncompromising martyr, and somehow unfit to tie Jesus' sandals. Setting aside Elijah's prophetic mantle for the redemptive Christ promised to Adam, John discards vain attempts to garner divine favour. John revels in grace, repudiating power in favour of messianic sacrifice, even in Herod's dungeon. A Gospel icon, John seizes the richness of submission and the blessing of a lesser state, squashing the crowd's sentiment that he might be the Christ. John, though near perfect, cannot wait to step aside in order to cast his lot with the Christ to whom he eagerly bows his head.

I WOULD BE WISE TO EXCHANGE MY PRIDEFUL INDEPENDENCE FOR JOHN'S GRACEFUL SUBSERVIENCE. In my actual weakness, Jesus necessarily serves as the protagonist in my biography, taking responsibility for securing my place with him. In light of John's admitted inadequacy to tie Jesus' sandals, should I presume to fasten the strings? I am no prophet, no Nazarene, no martyr, no maker of paths for messianic kings. I instead lie awake at night, imprisoned like Prometheus by my sin, suffering through memories of every unkind and wicked deed. If John needs the Lord, I need the Lord. If John steps aside, I should never even think to step up. As a first-class recalcitrant type, my Creative Memories book contains no montage of me opening the heavenly gate but only a single photograph of the Good Shepherd slinging my body, kicking and screaming over his shoulder as he carries me home.

Vince Woltjer and Tim Vandenberg, *To Be Honest With You*, Authentic Media, 2005

ReactionReactionReactionReaction

CIRCLE:

😊 ☹️ 😐 😠 😌 😲

TICK:

Total rubbish ☐   Not sure ☐   Worth thinking about ☐   Genius ☐

FILL:

....
....
....
....

Name: **Vanessa Green**

Age: **19**

Town: **Birmingham**

Current status: **Student / working for Saltmine Trust**

Passions: **Evangelism, youth work**

What is the greatest magazine in the world?

I love the free Asda magazine.

Cats or dogs?

Dogs. 110%. Big dogs.

Any siblings?

Yes, I have two sisters.

What is the most disgusting thing your sisters have ever done?

When we were little we used to do face masks and put cucumber on our eyes, and my sister used to eat the cucumber after it had been on my eyes.

What's the most gracious thing your dad's ever done for you?

I think because I'm the youngest I always get what I want. Sometimes he'll put money in my account if I need it. Also he gives hugs when I need it.

Reality Check

REWRITING AMAZING GRACE

John Newton wrote the original version of this well-known hymn in 1772. But in 2002, thebandwithnoname turned it into a rock/rap song and included it on their debut album *The Blitz*. Now it's your turn to bring it bang up to date by putting your own spin on the age-old theme of God's grace. It's sure to be a timeless classic . . .

TOP TIPS: Don't feel intimidated if you've never written a song before. Yours doesn't even have to have a tune! You may want to simply rewrite it line for line using a trusty dictionary and your own words. Or, for an added challenge, get your hands on a rhyming dictionary. Who knows? Once you've finished, your friends and family may be interested in a private performance!

Amazing Grace

Amazing grace! How sweet the sound
That saved a wretch like me!
I once was lost, but now am found;
Was blind, but now I see.

'Twas grace that taught my heart to fear,
And grace my fears relieved;
How precious did that grace appear
The hour I first believed.

Through many dangers, toils and snares,
I have already come;
'Tis grace hath brought me safe thus far,
And grace will lead me home.

The Lord has promised good to me,
His word my hope secures;
He will my shield and portion be,
As long as life endures.

Yes, when this flesh and heart shall fail,
And mortal life shall cease,
I shall possess, within the veil,
A life of joy and peace.

The world shall soon dissolve like snow,
The sun refuse to shine;
But God, who called me here below,
Shall be forever mine.

When we've been there ten thousand years,
Bright shining as the sun,
We've no less days to sing God's praise
Than when we'd first begun.

John Newton, 1772
Public Domain

The Father's Will

This is all there is in the world: wanting to please our sinful selves, wanting the sinful things we see and being too proud of what we have. But none of these comes from the Father. They come from the world. The world is passing away, and all the things that people want in the world are passing away. But whoever does what God wants will live forever.

(1 John 2:16–17)

First up

Have you ever wondered what Jesus was like as a teenager? We all know what he was like as a baby, and we remind ourselves of that every Christmas. We all know what happened when he was in his thirties; that's why we celebrate Easter. In fact, most of what we read about Jesus in the Bible is taken from when he was already a fully grown adult. But what about when he was a teenager? Did he ever get dumped by a girl? Did he ever get nervous before an important exam? Did he ever have acne?!

Even though the Bible is almost entirely silent on Jesus' teenage years (maybe he wanted it that way!) we are given a brief insight into what life was like for him at around the age of twelve. Here's a very important story that takes place during one unforgettable annual family visit to Jerusalem:

> Every year Jesus' parents went to Jerusalem for the Passover festival. When Jesus was twelve years old, they went to the festival as usual. When the festival was over, they went home, but Jesus stayed in Jerusalem. His parents did not know this. They travelled for a whole day thinking that Jesus was with them in the group. They began looking for him among their family and close friends, but they did not find him. So they went back to Jerusalem to look for him there.

> After three days they found him. Jesus was sitting in the Temple area with the religious teachers, listening and asking them questions. Everyone who heard him was amazed at his understanding and wise answers. When his parents saw him, they wondered how this was possible. And his mother said, 'Son, why did you do this to us? Your father and I were very worried about you. We have been looking for you.'

> Jesus said to them, 'Why did you have to look for me? You should have known that I must be where my Father's works.' But they did not understand the meaning of what he said to them.

> Jesus went with them to Nazareth and obeyed them. His mother was still thinking about all these things. As Jesus grew taller, he continued to grow in wisdom. God was pleased with him and so were the people who knew him.

(Luke 2:41–52)

The rest of this book will primarily focus on the Father's will. Jesus knew – even at an early age – that he was living his life according to someone else's agenda. He was about his Father's business, spending as much time as possible in his Father's house. This couldn't have made much sense to poor Mary and Joseph at the time, but eventually they would come to understand (along with the rest of us) that Jesus was following God's will for his life – perfectly. This became even clearer as the time approached for Jesus to die. He was alone in the garden of Gethsemane, and he cried out to God through blood, sweat and tears.

> He said, 'Abba, Father! You can do all things. Don't make me drink from this cup. But do what you want, not what I want.'
> (Mark 14:36)

As your loving, powerful, gracious heavenly Father, God has a perfect plan for all our lives. And if we're faithful to follow it wholeheartedly then, like Jesus, we too will be rewarded accordingly. We too can become wiser and find favour with God and people. God's will is his roadmap for us to find true success. Yours may not look like ours, but that's OK. That just means that God has made you to be unique. No one can be you the way you can be you. So be yourself. Be the 'you' that God intended you to be. Follow his will.

Name: Jamie Waite

Age: 16

Town: Sunderland

PEOPLE CLIP

Passions: Flying, Maths

Which animal best describes you?

Koala Bear.

Place you'd like to visit?

Cyprus.

Last time you had a really good memorable meal?

Two weeks ago. The Indian Tandoori on the way from Sunderland to Soul Survivor in Shepton Mallet.

How have you experienced God as a Father?

My mum is a single parent, so I actually have God as my Father. Whenever I try to tell her a lie, my heavenly Dad lets my earthly mum know.

How would you describe God as a dad to someone else?

He looks out for me in everything I do and guides me to do the right thing.

FATHER
through the years

4 years: My daddy can do anything.

7 years: My dad knows a lot, a whole lot.

8 years: My father doesn't quite know everything.

12 years: Oh well, naturally my father doesn't know everything.

14 years: Father? Hopelessly old-fashioned.

18 years: I know more than Dad.

21 years: Oh, that man is out of date. What did you expect?

25 years: He knows a little bit about it, but not much.

30 years: Must find out what Dad thinks about it.

35 years: A little patience; let's get Dad's ideas first.

50 years: What would Dad have thought about it?

60 years: My dad knew literally everything.

65 years: I wish I could talk it over with my dad once more.

(Author Unknown)

Father knows best

There have been times where as a parent you think you know what is right for your kids and what is best but they don't think the same. That starts as they get older. You have to let go so they can make the choice themselves. Letting go is often really difficult.

STEPS OF FAITH

chipK's mind

I can think if several key decisions in my life that have come only after prolonged times of seeking the Father for his perfect will.

T here was the time when I was a young teenager thinking about getting my ear pierced (it was a massive decision at the time!). Our family had spent three days in the Negev Desert in Israel, just getting alone with God and listening to his voice. The biggest consideration for me was that I didn't want to offend anyone in the international churches that our family would be ministering in, and I knew that being a young man and having my ear pierced might be seen as controversial. It wasn't until we got home from our desert experience that **I FINALLY RECEIVED A 'BREAKTHROUGH' BIBLE VERSE AND FELT THAT GOD WAS SAYING IT WOULD BE OK.**

Then there was an invitation for our youth group to travel from Israel to Slovakia on a mission trip. Anyone who felt God was leading them to go would have to raise their own money for the flights, so it was a pretty big decision. As I prayed about it, God gave me a vision. I could see footprints walking across a map, from Israel into Europe and back. When I checked out a real map, I found that the section of Europe I'd seen footprints stepping towards in my vision was in fact Slovakia. That trip proved to be a milestone in many ways for me personally, as well as for the rest of my youth group.

I could tell many similar stories: like making the decision to move to California to go to Bible College, or praying nearly every night for my future wife for as long as I can remember (right up until I found her, of course!), or deciding what God wanted me to do when thebandwithnoname finished. But in every single one of them, two vital components were there. Firstly, I had to wait on God for as long as it took. And secondly, I needed to eventually take a step of faith, even if it was just a small one.

As you seek the Father's will in every area of your life, be sure to carve out precious time to wait on him. And as you do, be prepared to do whatever he asks, even if it means taking a step of faith out of your comfort zone and into something new.

God's mind

The LORD watches over his followers,
those who wait for him to show his faithful love.
He saves them from death.
He gives them strength when they are hungry.
So we will wait for the LORD.
He helps us and protects us.
He makes us happy
because we trust him who alone is holy.

(Psalm 33:18–21)

Trust the LORD completely, and don't depend on your own
knowledge. With every step you take, think about what he
wants, and he will help you go the right way.

(Proverbs 3:5–6)

Peter said, 'Lord, if that is really you,
tell me to come to you on the water.'
Jesus said, 'Come, Peter.'
Then Peter left the boat and walked on the water to Jesus.

(Matthew 14:28–29)

ReactionReactionReactionReaction

CIRCLE:

TICK:

Total rubbish ☐   Not sure ☐   Worth thinking about ☐   Genius ☐

FILL:

....
....
....
....

Play Your Part

Helen talks

If you saw it, I'm sure you remember the opening ceremony for the Olympics in London during 2012. It was the most amazing show and totally blew the lid off everyone's expectations. It involved massive moving sets, farm animals, dancing nurses, giant smoke stack chimneys and a million other things. Hundreds, if not thousands, of dancers, actors and volunteers were part of the performance.

Apparently each volunteer had to do around 100 hours of rehearsals. What a commitment! With so many people in the show you can imagine those with smaller parts might have been tempted not to show up for all those rehearsals. But imagine the impact of that on the overall production. With so many interlocking scenes and set changes, costume changes, pyrotechnics and lighting cues, rehearsals would have become impossible if each person hadn't continued to play their part.

On a planet filled with 7 billion people it's easy to feel like a tiny, insignificant blip whose actions don't matter. According to the BBC News website* I am the **78,712,458,199th** person to have lived since history began! If anything will make you feel insignificant, numbers like that will. But despite this, **I KNOW THAT I AM NOT JUST A NUMBER.**

God designed each of us and has a role for each of us to play in his grand plan. Your part might be as a singer on the main stage or it might be an extra in the crowd, but without everyone doing what they are made to do the performance does not work. God designed you with a combination of talents, gifts, experience and opportunities that no one else has. He's also given you a unique set of desires and things that you love to do. All these things come together to equip you perfectly for the part God has designed for you. Make sure you don't spend too much time comparing yourself to others but instead spend lots of time listening to God about what part you should be playing.

Read Psalm 139:15–18 and then write down how well you think God knows you.

Spend some time dreaming about what you would love to do with your life and submitting those plans and ideas to God in prayer. Spend some time listening for his direction and part for you.

*(http://www.bbc.co.uk/news/world-15391515 on 11th Jan 2013)

CIRCLE:

😊 ☹️ 😐 😮 🙂 😲

TICK:

Total rubbish ☐   Not sure ☐   Worth thinking about ☐   Genius ☐

FILL:

....

....

Father knows best

God's strategy for dealing with rejection is quite different to ours. Ours is to draw boundaries and say, 'Well if you are going to do that then I am going to do this,' but God isn't like that. He makes himself vulnerable and makes it easier for us to cross boundaries to get back to him. A mature parent will choose not to view a rejection of his opinions as a rejection of his love.

Dear Rob,

You've probably never heard of 'Robbie the Flying Pyro', but when I was growing up he was one of my heroes. He was a motorbike stuntman who would come to our little town every summer, putting on a show that still lingers in my memory to this day. His stunts and tricks were world-class, and he always had time for us kids after each performance. He'd answer our questions and sign our posters, and all of us just knew that when we grew up we wanted to be like Robbie.

One year, my best friend and I decided to camp out right beside the Pyro's trailer. Talk about dedicated fans! The next morning, he was so impressed with us that he cleared his schedule in order to show us around all his gadgets and equipment. He led us meticulously through his exercise and practice routines, he took us behind the scenes and showed us how each stunt bike, cannon and prop machine worked, and he even gave us an exclusive sneak peek at some of the blueprints for his upcoming stunts that were still a work-in-progress.

I vividly remember one blueprint in particular that was covered from top to bottom in measurements, ratios, designs and predicted results. Up until that point I'd never imagined that so much thought and hard work went into a stunt that Robbie made appear so effortless. And somehow, at that moment, even at such a young age, I had a revelation about God.

I'd always heard that God had a plan for my life. I believed that somewhere out there, way beyond the cosmos, God was watching me . . . hoping I wouldn't get run over by a bus or something. But as I looked down at all those scribbled notes my hero had drawn, it suddenly occurred to me that my heavenly Father was genuinely interested in the tiniest detail of my everyday life. I realized his thoughts about me were too numerous to count. He knew every hair on my head and he designed me with the most incredible purposes in mind.

The reason I've written all this down for you is because I believe at some point in your life, you will have this same revelation. Maybe you've already had it. I might have big dreams for you, but God's dreams are way bigger than mine. His plan, his will, his design, his destiny, his blueprint . . . whatever you want to call it . . . can only be discovered by spending time with him. Wait for him. Camp out next to him if you have to! I promise you, it'll be worth the wait.

I love you forever,

Dad

Can God Use Me?

When I was 22, I established a mission in Cornwall called 'Dawn Patrol'. It was a mission to surfers primarily but also to clubbers, skaters and the wider party scene. As we were doing prep. for the mission, it dawned on me that we as a church had often been so busy 'doing' mission with creative and good ideas that we had in fact failed to listen to God!

herefore, on Dawn Patrol, though we put together a great programme of events, we were not tied to it. Each day of the mission we would pray and listen to hear the Father's perspective. Sometimes we scrapped entire parts of the programme to do what God wanted to do. It was not only the leadership group that spent time listening to God but **EVERY DELEGATE WAS ENCOURAGED TO SPEND TIME LISTENING**. As God spoke to individuals, the words were tested by the group and we saw great things happen.

It all stemmed from our relationship with God. For example, one team had two people who both separately felt quite sure that God was calling someone from the team to wait outside Woolworths. In faith, they sent out one of the team to stand there. He waited for an hour and then someone came up to him and said, 'Excuse me, you have been standing here for a long time – what are you waiting for?'

The team member explained the situation to the stranger and God opened up a door. The team member had an amazing conversation and explained the gospel. He even got to pray for the stranger outside Woolies!

A few team members from another team were working on the beach and felt that God was calling them to go and pray for healing for an Asian family. They wandered over to them, they were unsure what exactly needed prayer. As they chatted to the young people, one of them explained that he was in agony as he had been stung twice in the foot by a weaver fish. They offered to pray for healing and immediately the young guy was jumping up and down pain free. They then prayed for his brother who had his arm in a sling and who could not move his fingers. Again the brother felt the pain had gone and began moving his fingers. As a result the whole family came to Christ.

Andy Frost and Jo Wells, *Freestyle*, **Authentic Media, 2005**

ReactionReactionReactionReaction

CIRCLE:

😊 🙁 😐 😯 😌 😲

TICK:

Total rubbish ☐   Not sure ☐   Worth thinking about ☐   Genius ☐

FILL:

....
....
....
....

Father knows best

When your children head in a direction that is not sensible, you don't love them less but it's frustrating that they can't see that they are doing a stupid thing.

OBEDIENCE

chipK's mind

I believe there's one thing every young boy needs. A dog. Mine was called 'Buddy' (we named it after our pastor in Florida . . . he wasn't too happy about that . . . the pastor, that is), and Buddy was half cocker spaniel and half poodle. He was a 'cock-a-poo'. It was a big responsibility having a dog to walk and clean and feed, but the rewards certainly outweighed the burdens. He was always there to welcome me home, make me smile and cheer me up when I was grumpy. Buddy was especially fun to wind up. The mere mention of the word 'cat' would set him off barking, jumping and generally going berserk. Eventually, he even learned the word in Hebrew, 'khatool', and this too would drive him crazy. Ah, those were the days!

When he started to get old, Buddy really struggled with one essential quality. Obedience. Now don't get me wrong, it wasn't on purpose. He was the most faithful friend a boy could ask for. Buddy's disobedience was due to the fact that he was almost entirely deaf! In fact, not only was he deaf, he suffered from terribly poor eyesight and a nasty recurring skin disease. So when we'd call him over for his skin medicine, we'd have to shout just to get him to hear us. Then, when he finally heard us, because of his bad eyesight, **HE'D RUN IN THE OPPOSITE DIRECTION!**

The Bible tells a story about a guy called Jonah who kinda did the same thing to God. Only this dude wasn't blind or deaf. He knew without a doubt that God was calling him to go and preach in a town called Nineveh, but he desperately did not want to go. So, like Buddy, he went in the opposite direction. After getting swallowed by a massive fish, he eventually sorted things out with God and went to Nineveh.

Obeying God is always the right thing to do. It's even better than giving up everything for him. Ultimately he's got your best interests at heart, and he knows what you need better than you do. Listen and obey.

God's mind

Read the story of Jonah in Jonah 1 – 3

But Samuel answered, 'Which pleases the LORD more: burnt offerings and sacrifices or obeying his commands? It is better to obey the LORD than to offer sacrifices to him. It is better to listen to him than to offer the fat from rams.'
(1 Samuel 15:22)

Children, obey your parents the way the Lord wants, because this is the right thing to do. The command says, 'You must respect your father and mother.' This is the first command that has a promise with it. And this is the promise: 'Then all will go well with you, and you will have a long life on the earth.'
(Ephesians 6:1–3)

LORD, teach me your ways, and I will live and obey your truths. Help me make worshipping your name the most important thing in my life.
(Psalm 86:11)

Your mind

- **On a scale of 1–10, how good am I at obeying my parents?**

  1   2   3   4   5   6   7   8   9   10

- **Are there any circumstances in my life today in which I'm not being obedient to God?**

  ....
  ....

- **What happens when I disobey God?**

  ....
  ....

- **When was the last time I did something I shouldn't have done?**

  ....
  ....

- **What is God calling me to do now?**

....

....

- **I will be obedient by:**

....

....

Chip Kendall, *The Mind of chipK: Enter at Your Own Risk*, Authentic Media, 2006

ReactionReactionReactionReaction

CIRCLE:

☺ ☹ 😐 😮 😕 😲

TICK:

Total rubbish ☐   Not sure ☐   Worth thinking about ☐   Genius ☐

FILL:

....

....

Father knows best

As a parent you put opportunities in front of your kids and then support them through the choices they make. You help them do things they enjoy, facilitate it and help to make it possible.

Not My Will

Chip talks

A missionary steps into a remote jungle on the other side of the world; a place notorious for making martyrs of people who dare to share their faith with its inhabitants . . .

Father, do what you want, not what I want.

A secret believer in communist China stands before a firing squad and listens to the commander's ultimatum: 'Deny Christ and go free, or follow him to your death' . . .

Father, do what you want, not what I want.

A man prays alone in a garden, sweating drops of blood, faced with his most fearsome challenge yet – the ultimate sacrifice for the sins of the world. He turns his head heavenward towards his Father . . .

Father, do what you want, not what I want.

t's easy to serve God and call yourself a Christian when everything around you is going well. You're comfortable. You have everything you need. People come to you for advice because you're living the life they want. But this isn't necessarily the life that Jesus promised us. He said, 'Remember the lesson I told you: servants are not greater than their master. **IF PEOPLE TREATED ME BADLY, THEY WILL TREAT YOU BADLY TOO.** And if they obeyed my teaching, they will obey yours too. They will do to you whatever they did to me, because you belong to me. They don't know the one who sent me' (John 15:20–21). Jesus also said, 'If any of you want to be my follower, you must stop thinking about yourself and what you want. You must be willing to carry the cross that is given to you for following me. Any of you who try to save the life you have will lose it. But you who give up your life for me will find true life' (Matthew 16:24–25).

I often think about the rich young ruler's encounter with Jesus (read the entire account in Mark 10:17–27 if you're not already familiar with the story). It's so different to the way a lot of modern-day evangelists do things. Here you have a guy who honestly wants to be Jesus' follower, and Jesus doesn't lead him in a simple prayer or even give the poor guy a hug. Instead, he throws down the gauntlet. He forces him to genuinely count the cost of discipleship, and when the young man can't agree to Jesus' terms, Jesus lets him walk away.

Choosing God's will over your own is a personal decision that no one else can make for you. It may not always look like the most practical or desirable option, but history proves over and over again that it is always the right decision to make. **OUR HEAVENLY FATHER LOVES US.** He designed us to function in a certain way. He's always got our best interests at heart, and once we begin to see things from an eternal perspective, we'll begin to realize that our frustration and pain are only temporary. We, like Jesus, can learn to say, 'Do what you want, not what I want.'

Further reading:

- *Mark 10:28–31*
- *John 17:14–19*
- *Romans 5:3–5*
- *Mark 10:28–31*

ReactionReactionReactionReaction

CIRCLE:

TICK:

Total rubbish ☐ Not sure ☐ Worth thinking about ☐ Genius ☐

FILL:

....

....

....

....

Here's the plan...

Helen talks

Try to imagine the following scenario and think about how it makes you feel.

On the day you turn 18, your loving parents sit you down and explain their plan for your life. To them, it makes perfect sense that they should do this. After all, they have known you longer than anyone else and they love you and want what's best for you. They also have the advantage of having lived longer, and from experience know some of the lessons and pitfalls they can help you avoid. Surely they are far better equipped to plan your life than you. It goes something like this . . .

They've researched universities and decided that Leeds Metropolitan is the best one for you and that you should study Events Management. You should attend that university for three years and New Life Church would be a great place for you to worship while you are there.

They explain that after you complete your degree you should move to London and get a job with a company called Live Events, based in Fulham. Incidentally Fulham is where the child of one of their oldest friends lives, and they've decided you two would be good together. You are instructed to start a relationship with them after 6 months of moving to the area, and aim to get married around two years later. After this you should both leave your jobs and begin work for a Christian ministry running evangelistic outreach events in South America. After some years helping to develop the ministry you should move to Brazil for a year before coming back to the UK and starting a family.

Like the sound of this?

Now, this might be a great plan. It might even be a plan that would make you happy, but **DOES ANYONE ELSE FEEL COMPLETELY HORRIFIED AND TRAPPED BY THE THOUGHT OF THIS CONVERSATION?** Or is it just me?

It's horrible to imagine your life mapped out ahead of you without you being part of the decision-making process, even if it has all been done with your best interests at heart, by people who love you. But these are all things that we sometimes wish our Father God would spell out his plan for. 'Where should I go to university?' 'Who should I marry?' 'Where should I live?' 'What ministry am I called to?' Sometimes it feels as if it would be nice to know exactly what to do and exactly what God has got for us in the future, but fortunately God tends to show us step by step.

I THINK GOD WANTS TO TAKE US ON AN ADVENTURE WITH HIM. HE DOESN'T WANT TO JUST GIVE US A LIST OF INSTRUCTIONS, because then we wouldn't have to keep asking him 'What next?' and getting close enough to hear the answer. It's often more of a treasure hunt or paper chase than a pre-explained plan, but he leads us to one place and then opens up the next opportunity from there. Looking back, it becomes clear that he has been the one leading us all the way.

- *What are you asking God for direction for at the moment?*
- *Take some time to thank God that he has a great plan for your life and to ask him for the next step.*

People can plan what they want to do, but it is the LORD who guides their steps.
(Proverbs 16:9)

'I have good plans for you. I don't plan to hurt you. I plan to give you hope and a good future.'
(Jeremiah 29:11)

ReactionReactionReactionReaction

CIRCLE:

TICK:

Total rubbish ☐   Not sure ☐   Worth thinking about ☐   Genius ☐

FILL:

....

....

....

....

Name: **Ruth Donaldson**

Age: **19**

Town: **Oxford**

Current status: **Youth and Student ministries – Open Doors**

Passion: **Persecuted church**

How many countries have you visited?

Six so far.

What two sentences would you say to the whole world if you could?

Jesus Christ rocks and is our saviour. Jesus Christ wants to save you.

Do you prefer green or blue?

Blue.

Earliest childhood memory?

I have vivid and scratched memories of me being on a tricycle when I was two.

If your dad wants you to do something, does he ever tell you that without using words?

My dad has a funny way, he's very sarcastic, sometimes he really communicates through movements and actions.

Name one thing that your heavenly Dad wants you to do, but right now you don't want to do it.

I think it's so easy to be comfortable here in the UK. I am passionate about the persecuted church, but if God's telling me to go to Iran or Iraq and sacrifice my life, I don't know if I would do that.

Reality Check

DAD GIVES THE BEST GIFTS

Did you know that everything truly good in your life ultimately comes from your Dad in heaven? 'Everything good comes from God. Every perfect gift is from him. These good gifts come down from the Father who made all the lights in the sky. But God never changes like the shadows from those lights. He is always the same' (James 1:17). Some translations actually refer to him as the *father* of lights.

Why not take the next few minutes to think about the gifts God has given you and thank him for them. Meditate on each one and try to work out for yourself if and how each one has ultimately come from your heavenly Dad. Here's a list to kick start your brain, but feel free to add on more!

Jesus

Holy Spirit

friends

parents / brothers and sisters

church community

teachers / leaders

shelter

food

Bible

body / senses

health / warmth

talents / unique abilities

music

money

favourite possessions

sport

pets

freedom

pictures

eternal life / knowing God

entertainment

hobbies / free time

books

laughter / tears

role models

transportation

dreams / ideas

promises for the future

all of creation!

Pray

Father, we thank you because you have been the one carrying our readers all the way through this study guide. We praise you because you are faithful to complete the incredible work you've begun in them. Continue to reveal your love, power, grace and will to the one reading this right now, and help them to obey you as their heavenly Dad. When they're going through difficult times, show them just how close you are – as close as their next breath. When they're sitting on top of the world, remind them to give you the credit because every good and perfect gift really does come from you, Father. Most of all, our prayer is that you would use the knowledge gained from this book to shape this precious reader into the best spiritual parent they can be, so they can pass it on to others who look up to them. Make all of us more like you.

We love you, Dad.

In Jesus' name,

Amen.

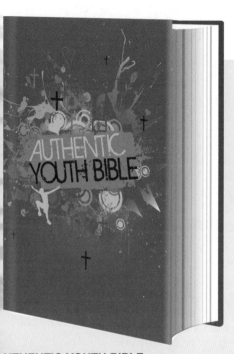